Early Explorers

Written by Ellen Kavanagh

Rourke
Educational Media

rourkeeducationalmedia.com

*Scan for Related Titles
and Teacher Resources*

www.rourkeeducationalmedia.com

PHOTO CREDITS: Cover & title page: © howard Oates: © Illustrious, © javarman3; page 5: © JeanUrsula; page 6: © yorkfoto, © rimglow; page 7: © wikipedia; page 8: © wikipedia; page 9:© raclro; page 10: © wikimedia; page 11: © Eugenio Opitz, © AVvector; page 13: © wikimedia; page 14: © wikipedia; page 15: © HultonArchive; page 17: © wikimedia; page 18: © Jelen80; page 19: © rramirez125; page 21

Edited by: Jill Sherman

Cover: Tara Raymo

Interior design by: Pamela McCollum

Library of Congress PCN Data

Early Explorers / Ellen Kavanagh
(Little World Social Studies)
ISBN 978-1-62169-918-7 (hard cover)(alk. paper)
ISBN 978-1-62169-813-5 (soft cover)
ISBN 978-1-62717-023-9 (e-Book)
Library of Congress Control Number:2013937312

Also Available as:

ROURKE'S
e-Books

Rourke Educational Media
Printed in the United States of America,
North Mankato, Minnesota

Rourke
Educational Media

rourkeeducationalmedia.com

customerservice@rourkeeducationalmedia.com • PO Box 643328 Vero Beach, Florida 32964

Table of Contents

Exploring the World

Explorers are people who visit and study unknown lands. The early explorers traveled across oceans and continents to make **maps** of the shape and size of the Earth.

The early explorers were very courageous and had a spirit for adventure. Their explorations gave us new knowledge about our Earth.

Eric the Red (950 AD–1003)

Eric the Red, a Viking explorer, set sail in 981 from Iceland and discovered Greenland. In 986, he took 500 Viking people in 25 ships to build a new Viking colony called Brattahlid.

GREENLAND

● **Brattahlid**

The Viking people fished and trapped animals to earn a living in Brattahlid, Greenland.

Marco Polo (1254–1324)

Marco Polo was an explorer from Venice, Italy. He made a living by trading **goods** with China. He traveled to many new lands from 1275 to 1292 to find new goods to **trade**.

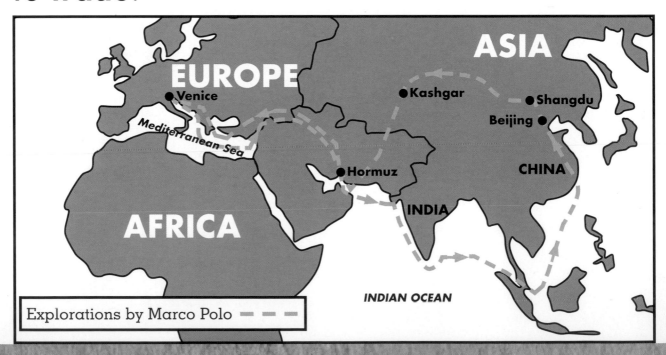

Explorations by Marco Polo – – –

Marco Polo wrote about his travels and described the paper money and postal systems used in China for trade. These writings excited people about exploration.

Christopher Columbus (1451–1506)

Christopher Columbus, an Italian explorer, set out with his three ships in 1492 to chart a new **ocean** route from Spain to Asia. Instead of landing in Asia, he landed in the Caribbean. He did not realize that he had found a new **continent**!

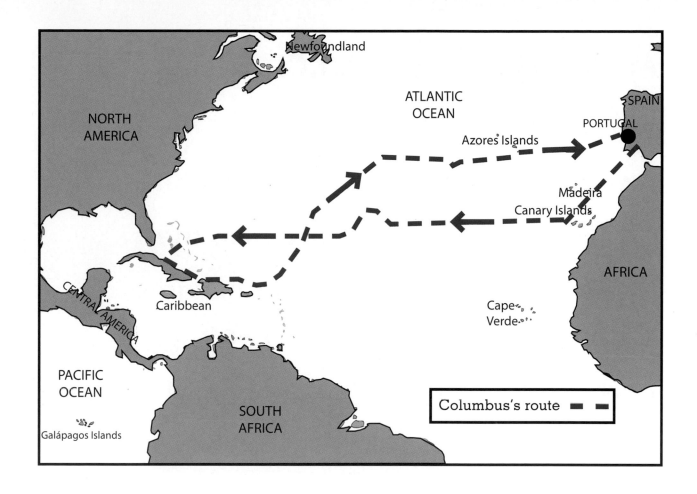

Columbus crossed the Atlantic Ocean from Spain with his three ships, the *Niña*, the *Pinta*, and the *Santa María*. He landed in the Caribbean on October 12, 1492.

Amerigo Vespucci
(1451–1512)

America was named for the Italian explorer Amerigo Vespucci. He met Christopher Columbus, and became interested in exploring. In 1497, he crossed the Atlantic Ocean to find South America.

Amerigo Vespucci found the coast of Venezuela. He finally realized that he was not in Asia, but on a separate land. This new continent was named "America" in his honor.

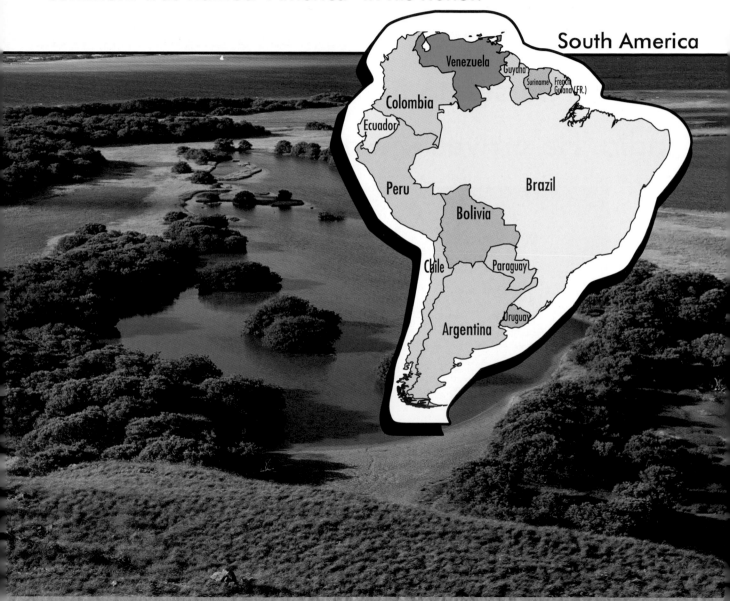

South America

Venezuela
Guyana
Suriname
French Guiana (FR.)
Colombia
Ecuador
Peru
Brazil
Bolivia
Chile
Paraguay
Uruguay
Argentina

Vasco da Gama (1460–1524)

Vasco da Gama, a Portuguese explorer, was the first person to find a sailing route to India. He arrived in Calicut, India, in 1498.

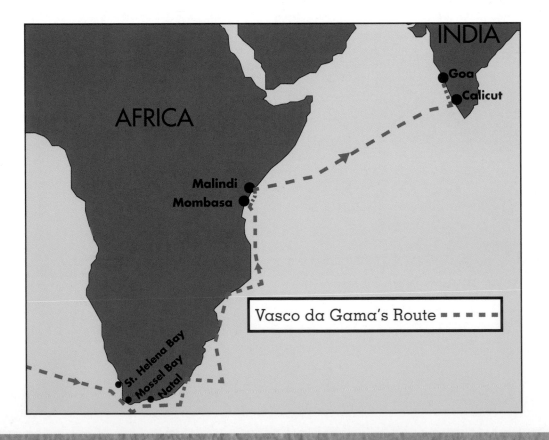

Vasco da Gama was the first European to set up many trade posts after arriving in India.

Vasco Núñez de Balboa
(1475–1519)

Vasco Núñez de Balboa, a Spanish explorer, sailed across the Atlantic Ocean to South America in 1511. He settled in Panama. Balboa heard stories that another ocean was located to the west of Panama and set out to find it in 1513.

CENTRAL AMERICA

Panama

Balboa reached a large body of water, which was later named the Pacific Ocean. He claimed it for the King of Spain.

Ferdinand Magellan (1480–1521)

Ferdinand Magellan, a Portuguese explorer, led the first journey around the world. In September 1519, he led 5 ships out of Spain and crossed the Atlantic Ocean to Brazil. Then he sailed south around South America.

MAGELLAN'S VOYAGE

Magellan then sailed north through the Pacific Ocean. He stopped at the Philippine Islands where he was killed. Magellan's ship, the *Victoria*, continued back to Spain in 1522. *Victoria* was the first ship to sail around the world.

Magellan named the Pacific Ocean. He called it "Pacific" because the ocean was peaceful and calm with gentle, mild winds.

These explorers were the first to explore unknown oceans and continents. They discovered new trade routes and goods that we still use today.

Picture Glossary

continent (KON-tuh-nuhnt): A continent is one of the seven large land masses of the Earth. The continents are Asia, Africa, Europe, North America, South America, Australia, and Antarctica.

explorers (ek-SPLOR-urz): An explorer is a person who travels in order to discover a new place.

goods (GUDZ): Goods are things that are sold, or things that someone owns, such as leather goods or household goods.

maps (MAPS): A map is a detailed plan of an area, showing features such as oceans, rivers, and mountains.

ocean (OH-shuhn): An ocean is a large body of salt water. The main oceans of the world are the Pacific Ocean, Atlantic Ocean, Indian Ocean, Arctic Ocean, and Southern Ocean.

trade (TRADE): Trade is the business of buying and selling goods.

Index

Websites

www.socialstudiesforkids.com/subjects/explorers.htm

allaboutexplorers.com

www.kidinfo.com/american_history/explorers.html

About the Author

Ellen Kavanagh has been teaching four and five year olds since 1995. She and her family love reading all sorts of books!

Meet The Author!
www.meetREMauthors.com